SPELLING GAMES AND ACTIVITIES

CONTENTS

	Page
Introduction	5
Why games and activities	6
The important features of good spelling	7
Spelling in the National Curriculum	8
Introduction to the games and activities	10
Parents and home-school liaison	11
Stages in spelling	13
Stage 1 Pre-communicative	14
Early 'pre-spelling' games and activities	15
Rhymes A Oral rhymes	15
B Rhyming sets	16
Memory activities A Auditory memory	20
B Visual memory	
& discrimination	22
Stage 2 Semi-phonemic	27
The beginning of phonic awareness and early core	
sight spelling vocabularies games and activities	28
Sight words	29
Letter names	33
Letter sounds	36
Stage 3 Phonemic	38
Getting prepared for sounds games and activities	40
Spelling by sounds	40

Stage 4 Transitional 47

Activities to help children become aware of the
visual make-up of words 49

Spelling by sight memory 50

Stage 5 Correct 54

Becoming proficient at spelling games and
activities 55

Becoming more proficient at spelling 56

Conclusion 58

References 61

Resources and Further Reading 63

Introduction

The intention of this book is to give information about extra games and activities to supplement and consolidate the spelling teaching programme. It is not about methods of learning to spell although some of these will be mentioned in passing. Therefore, the initial programme and the appropriate teaching-cum-learning strategy is the province of the teacher.

This book, therefore, is designed to lead teachers to various ideas for supplementing children's learning at particular stages of spelling acquisition. It expects the teacher to have determined where the children are placed in the acquisition of spelling and what kind of learners they might be.

Teachers will for their part act in partnership with parents and pass on relevant ideas for home activities. Also parents will return information about their children's progress to the school.

The games and activities are not described in full detail. They are outlined. Because adults know their children better than any writer does, they are better aware of what particular form the activity or game should take. They know their own resources, both human and material.

The message should be **enjoy spelling**. The more children are given freedom to experiment, the more competent at spelling they will become. Being able to spell easily should lead to an enjoyment of writing creatively as it liberates the learner from the more difficult secretarial skills of spelling.

Why games and activities

Games and allied activities are most important at giving the learners a strong basis upon which to build their spelling skills. They are probably one of the best methods of learning to spell. They should help to consolidate the learning process that is being taught. Parents can undertake many of the ideas given later without feeling the tension which is often aroused when helping their children with spellings. Games can overcome the tedium and boredom that can arise if learning has to be undertaken in extremely small stages. Games may be motivating, as learners can compete against themselves or their peers. Given an interesting game or activity at the correct level, a child can achieve success and therefore become confident. Many weak spellers have very low self-esteem and need to be guided gently into the learning process.

Games cannot and, therefore, should not replace learning how to learn to spell. They should supplement parts of the learning process when this is thought necessary. Any game undertaken should be checked to see that it is doing what is intended and everyone concerned should understand the purpose of the game.

Although there are no age levels set against these games and activities, it could be stated that those given for spelling stages 1 and 2 are primarily for Key Stage 1, those for spelling stages 3 and 4 are for Key Stage 2 and those directed at spelling stages 4 and 5 are for Key Stage 3. It must be emphasised that children differ in their requirements and some older children, especially those with specific learning difficulties, may need to understand quite basic activities to fill in an unlearned piece of knowledge.

The important features of good spelling

If we are to spell correctly some sense has to be made of the English spelling system. For words to be accepted as correct we have to write the letters in their correct order according to the accepted convention in English spelling of today. However, words can be communicable if this order is incorrect. We can read words with letters omitted or incorrectly sequenced, e.g. *the elphnt and his keepr haev been fro a wlk.* We can even decipher quite strange letter combinations, e.g. *my car crsht into the gararjz and mayd mudth damigje.* But these are not accurate and unfortunately would lose marks in external examinations. Key Stage 1 in the English National Curriculum includes a spelling test for seven-year-olds so from the early years of education children are made aware of the necessity of accuracy in spelling.

Also, in order to spell correctly, the learner has to be able to look at a particular word and commit its pattern to memory. This is particularly necessary with words that are irregular, such as *said* and *who.*

The learner also has to listen to the word and remember how it sounds. There are many words that contain regular sound patterns which never change, such as the *ing* string.

Both the visual and auditory memories have to work together in order to recall what is seen and what is heard. Here words which could have two or more sound patterns have to be reinforced by sight memory recognition, such as *pear, pare* and *pair.*

And then it is most essential that the remembered word can be written whenever it is needed. This memory recall plus its successful writing has to become an automatic process so that written work can be fluent without ideas being impeded by retrieval of spellings. If anyone who writes has to concentrate on the procedure of how to compose a word then the spontaneity of language will suffer and often a word that is easier to spell will be substituted.

If learners have difficulty with remembering what words look like, they have poor visual memories. They will often only use sounds to try unknown spellings. If learners have similar difficulties remembering what words sound like, it is their auditory memories which are at fault and they will try to learn words visually. If both are weak then the learner has no obvious approach to fall back on and often their attempts will be uncommunicable. Many children with specific spelling difficulties produce words that are bizarre and cannot be easily deciphered and read.

As mentioned earlier, the following activities and games are not age-dependant but rather stage-dependant (see pages 13, 14, 27, 38, 47 and 54) and, therefore, have to be adapted to best meet the stage and interest of the learner.

The game and the child must be well matched. At times strengths must be consolidated. At other times we need to help children overcome their difficulties.

Spelling in the National Curriculum

A brief summary of the requirements of National Curriculum spelling will be outlined and their relation to the developmental stages in spelling acquisition will be detailed in later sections. The summary will be repeated so that the reader can check the children's stage development against the National Curriculum spelling requirements. These are taken from the National Curriculum Orders produced by the School Curriculum and Assessment Authority (SCAA) in 1994.

Key Stage 1
'... Pupils should be taught to:
- write each letter of the alphabet;
- use their knowledge of sound-symbol relationships and phonological patterns;
- recognise and use simple spelling patterns;
- write common letter strings within familiar and common words;
- spell commonly occurring simple words;
- spell words with common prefixes and suffixes'.

'Pupils should be taught to check the accuracy of their spelling, and to use word books and dictionaries, identifying initial letters as the means of locating words. They should be given opportunities to experiment with the spelling of complex words and to discuss misapplied generalisations and other reasons for misspellings. Close attention should be paid to word families'.

Key Stage 2

'... Pupils should be accumulating a bank of words that they can spell correctly, and should be taught to check spellings and meanings of words, using dictionaries where appropriate. When looking up words, pupils should be taught to apply their knowledge of initial and subsequent letters and the organisation of dictionaries, including headings, abbreviations and other conventions. They should be taught:
- the meaning, use, and spelling of common prefixes and suffixes;
- the relevance of word families, roots and origins of words;
- alternative ways of writing the same sound;
- the spelling of words with inflectional endings'.
'Pupils should be taught to:
- spell complex, polysyllabic words which conform to regular patterns, and to break long and complex words into more manageable units, by using their knowledge of meaning and word structure.
- memorise the visual patterns of words, including those which are irregular;
- recognise silent letters;
- use the apostrophe to spell shortened forms of words;
- use appropriate terminology, including vowel and consonant'.

Key Stages 3 and 4

'... Pupils should be helped to increase their knowledge of regular patterns of spelling, word families, roots of words and their derivations. They should be taught to spell increasingly complex polysyllabic words that do not conform to regular patterns, and to proof read their writing carefully to check for errors using dictionaries where appropriate. Pupils should be given opportunities to develop discrimination in relation to other complexities in spelling, including heteronyms, e.g. *minute, lead, wind* and sight rhymes, e.g. *tough, dough'*.

Introduction to the games and activities

The games and activities are outlined according to the stages (see pages 14, 27, 38, 47 and 54) with suggested ways in which to overcome those difficulties which some children will experience as they learn to spell. These suggestions are not new. Many of them will be found in books in the school. What has been done is to try to group them into a logical order and to make as full a collection as possible.

Some of the games and activities need no prior preparation. However, others require some 'making'. One suggestion is that parents could be enrolled to help here. Many parents would like to become involved with their child's schooling and learning and if card or board games need sticking and cutting then parents can form a workshop for this. Not only does this become a social occasion but also it becomes a learning experience for adults and enhances home-school links. Remember that the parents should be able to play the games with their (or other) children either at school or at home in order to see the beneficial effects that these bring. If it is not the school's policy to ask parents to help in school then maybe there would be ancillary helpers or older pupils who could undertake these tasks.

If the classroom ancillaries make the games, it may be possible for them to use them with pupils as extra activities within the classroom. Or the games can be sent home for out-of-school activities. Any game or activity that has to be made up should be as 'kidproof' and weatherproof as possible. If games can be covered by see-through film or stored in plastic wallets their lives will be lengthened. Some Professional Development Centres have laminating facilities which would enhance the look of anything home-made and also prolong its life.

Any game or activity, whether it is a card or board game or a set of suggestions on a worksheet, should be set out and printed as 'professionally' as possible. Children deserve good quality materials. If possible illustrations should be included and coloured paper is more acceptable than white. However, coloured paper sometimes poses a problem for photocopying as a lighter setting may need to be used.

Teachers must be prepared to accept loss and damage if the games and activities go home. Teachers should want these activities to be enjoyed and therefore well used.

There are some activities that involve groups and some that are solo performances. If children embark on the latter then an adult must be prepared to see the result, to 'mark' the work and to talk through the activity. Praise should always be given. Competitive-type games should never become too competitive or some children will be faced with failure again and again. This point is particularly relevant where children with emotional and behavioural problems are concerned as these children often find it very difficult to be failures or losers.

Parents and home-school liaison

If these games and activities are to form part of the home-school practice then parents must be given some advice about how to help and use the games and activities most effectively. If it is possible then the whole family should be involved. However, if there is a child with a spelling problem who cannot cope with a younger or older sibling being more able than they are at a particular activity, the parents must be aware and extra sympathetic to this fact. It could be that the child with the problem will need some time of individual help which is solely for them.

Teachers should not assume that parents know what to do or can understand the written instructions with absolute clarity. Also there are some parents who have neither the time nor the inclination to undertake any work at home. If this is so then those children should not be

11

penalised. They should be given similar help in school from other adults if this can be arranged. All games and activities must be well and carefully explained so that any adult involved can understand the objectives.

Points for both parents and teachers to bear in mind when setting up a home-school programme are the following.

School
1. *Teachers* should always emphasise the positive side of the activity.
2. *Teachers* must show interest in the outcome of the home-school work. Notes should be made of what has been undertaken. Praise is most important.
3. Parents know their children. *Teachers* must listen to what the parents say about how the child is learning or not learning and must be prepared to change activities on parental advice.
4. Make sure that the games and activities fit the particular child and family. Be aware of any constraints there might be for undertaking what is sent home. *Teachers* should explain the nature and purpose of the games.

Home
1. The sessions should not clash with something else of interest. *What child would want to spell when a favourite TV programme is being watched by others in the next room? Parents* must be sensitive to this.
2. The time at home must not be one of stress. Sessions should be as pressure-free as possible. *Parents* should be helped to keep calm and not to panic. If stress and tension are built up then the work will have no effect. Unfortunately there are some parents who cannot cope with working with their own child because their own anxieties are transmitted and working relationships break down.
3. *Parents* should always emphasise the positive nature of the activity and give praise when it is due.
4. 'Little and often' should be a catch-phrase. This can be translated to working with the child for about five to ten minutes only - unless the

child asks for more. This will be far more effective than a long, hard, serious session. *Parents* should be aware of this.

5. *Parents* must understand that they may not see any immediate improvement in their children's spelling ability. Many of the activities are to make children more aware of the make-up of words rather than to bring about an instant change in the spelling side to written work.

6. *Parents* know their children. They should feel able to talk to the teachers about the benefits or otherwise of the games and activities. Teachers must listen to what the parents say about how the child is learning or not learning and must be prepared to change activities on parental advice.

Presentation

1. Keep all instructions as simple as possible and make them easy to understand. Do not make complicated rules.

2. All board or paper games should be attractively set out and easy to read. Well-printed words are better for reading than handwritten ones.

Stages in spelling

In addition to ways or methods of learning, it has been suggested that there are five stages in spelling acquisition (Gentry, 1981). Learners pass through these in order to become accurate at spelling. These are not mutually exclusive, as children can be using spelling strategies found in more than one of these stages. This theory of developmental spelling was researched during the 1980s when it was recognised that children passed through quite definite developmental stages as their writing became more developed. Although it is recognised that the visual element is of utmost importance for complete spelling acquisition, the stages format should not be ignored. For more details about spelling acquisition linking the different theories, the book *Spelling in Context* (Peters and Smith, 1993) is a useful publication.

Children can be found working over two or even three stages. The aim should be for children to try for themselves, to take risks, to become adventurous and to be confident enough to make errors. Spelling should be an interesting act of discovery rather than a chore which has to result in total accuracy at all times. The weekly spelling test, although a useful activity for those pupils who have adequate to good memories, often results in those with poor spelling abilities gaining low scores or learning only for the test.

Stage 1
Pre-communicative

This can be thought of as 'pre-spelling' where children understand why there are words and writing in their world. When they attempt to write it is often a type of 'play' writing, or 'scribble' writing, where adults cannot decipher the intended messages and where letters and random marks are side by side on the page. But children should be encouraged to create these messages and should be praised and congratulated for doing so.

Figure 1

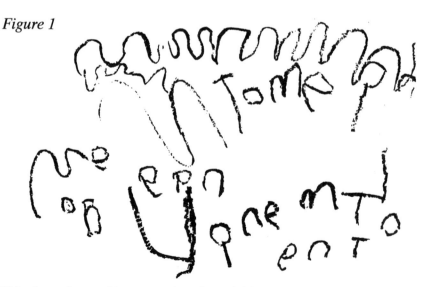

This piece of pre-writing was written by a child in a nursery class.

The Figure 1 example shows that this young writer is experimenting with both letters and patterns. He appears to know the difference between writing and drawing and in this piece of work there are no numbers alongside the letters. There are some actual letters and some words have appeared (e.g. *Tom, go, one?)* whether these are intentional or not.

Early 'pre-spelling' games and activities

The suggestions here complement many of those found for early reading and for helping to improve concentration and memory. They are the activities that can be observed in early years' classrooms and many need no preparation in terms of worksheets etc. If games are compiled and filed, teachers will be able to draw on activities for any part of this early spelling process. Most of the activities can be played in the home. Without this strong early foundation many children may have later problems with their written work.

Rhymes

AIM To enable children to become aware of rhyme in their language as this will give them a basis for the later understanding of words that can be spelt by using known sound patterns.

A. *Oral rhymes*

1. Help children to learn, repeat and chant *nursery rhymes* or *jingles*. Use hand or glove puppets so that the children can perform through these. Encourage the children to teach others. Use TV jingles and slogans with older pupils.

2. Many of these nursery rhymes or jingles are suitable for *playground games*.

> e.g. Ring-a-ring a *roses*
> A pocket full of *posies*

The actions serve to reinforce the rote-learning of the words, helping the words to be fixed in the child's memory.

3. Once the commonly known rhymes are learned then it is time to be more creative. Use your *own variations* with children supplying a word (either real or nonsense) that rhymes.

> e.g. Humpty Dumpty sat on a hill
>   Humpty Dumpty felt very ill

4. Another variation is *oral poems*. Encourage the children to complete very short rhymes. You will need a stock of these.

> e.g. We have fun,   I will buy
>   When we (run).   an apple (pie)
>   Going to get   I will throw it
>   A currant (bun)   in the (sky)

Many children's poetry books contain short amusing verses which can be learnt or used as examples.

5. Often children like *nonsense rhyming words* or words that sound like their own names. Enliven journeys or wet afternoons by producing examples and encouraging the child to give the rhyming word. These can also be put into poems or sentences. In school compile class poem books.

> e.g. *Alice* and *palace* (real word).
>   A girl called *Alice*
>   lived in a *palace.*
>   *Clive* and *dive* (real word)
>   When *Clive* was *five*
>   he learned how to *dive.*
>
>   *Jennifer* and *hennifer* (nonsense word).

B. *Rhyming sets*

In these activities children are linking the sounds they can hear spoken with actual objects or pictures of objects. At a later stage they will be more able to transfer this skill to words they speak and read and ultimately spell.

16

Once you have made your collection of items and games you will
have a ready store of activities for any necessary occasion.

1. *Rhyming picture cards*. Prepare pictures and mount them on cards.
   Get the children to say the names of the items and place them
   together according to their sounds.

2. ***Objects that rhyme***. Find actual objects that can be handled. Use PE hoops as sets to contain the objects. Make this into a team game or a sorting game where each hoop has to hold objects with different sounds.

3. Children can play ***rhyming snap*** with cards containing familiar pictorial objects. Make sure that the children name each picture and say the rhyming pair names together before they are allowed to keep the set. Or ask the children at the end of the game to say their pair names.

4. Another variant is ***rhyming lotto (simple)***. Make a board with 16 spaces for pictures. Choose four sounds with four pictures per sound such as short 'a' and 'i', 'ar' and long 'i' with pictures of *hat, rat, mat, cat, star, car, bar, tar, fin, tin, bin, chin, pie, sky, eye, sty.*

Give the two or four players their set of 16 cards (making sure that at least four of their cards are either blanks or other pictures), and in turn they match the pictures as the caller says the words. A rhyming set wins but the player has to say the words so that the sound element is reinforced. (There are many ways of playing this.)

5. *Rhyming lotto (next stage)*. Make a board with 16 spaces for pictures, with each picture containing a different sound. Each player has a set of different pictures containing the sounds on the board. The children have to match their picture with one on the board that rhymes.

BE CAREFUL

It should be noted that whenever pictures are used the children should be able to recognise and name them correctly. Go through the materials with the children before the game is played. A *hat* must not be a *cap* or vice versa; a *mat* must not be recognised as a *carpet*. Delete or change materials if any seem to confuse the players. It is most important that in any oral game the teacher or adult should be there to check that the children are using the materials correctly.

Memory activities

AIM Any activity or game involving children's 'hearing' memory will help their skills of listening, concentration, remembering, recalling and any subsequent action that is required. Any activity or game involving children's 'seeing' memory is intended to improve their powers of observation and recall of what they have seen.

A. *Auditory memory*

There are many listening games and activities which are devised to make the children more aware of sounds that are the same and sounds that are different, and to remember and use particular sounds.

1. *Sounds round about*. Ask the children either in class or at home to listen for, and remember, all the sounds they can hear either inside or outside the room over a short period of time (30 seconds would be appropriate). They should be encouraged to identify and locate these sounds.

2. *Common sounds*. Play taped sounds of everyday occurrences for identification.

20

3. ***Differences in sounds***. Encourage children to tell the difference between sounds. Get them to listen for high and low sounds, soft and loud sounds and similar sounds at different pitches. (Musical instruments can be used for this. For example, two water glasses with variable depths of water can be struck.)

4. ***Beating and counting sounds***. Tap out a rhythm and ask the child to repeat this. Another version is for the child to count the number of taps heard. (This activity will help later work on multi-syllabic words.)

5. ***Reacting to stories***. Tell a story. Ask the children to be on the lookout for a particular type of word (e.g. colours, fruit, animals) and when they hear one they should react in some way (e.g. clap, stand up).

   e.g. It was a very hot day and the sun was *gold* in the *blue* sky. The brother and sister walked slowly along the *grey* dusty road which was shaded by pale *green* trees. Ben was hot so he took off his *fawn* jumper and stuffed it into his *purple* carrier bag. 'I'm not as hot as you,' said Linda. 'I'm wearing my *pink* sun hat.' Ben and Linda were walking to the village to post a letter. It seemed a long way. A small *brown* bird cheeped in the bushes and a *white* sheep could be seen asleep in a field. As they got nearer to the village the sun made the road seem *yellow.*

   Stories like this take very little time to prepare and once done can be used time and time again. Record these on tape or make a written collection.

6. ***Listening in teams***. Arrange the children in teams. If a colour story was told then each team would colour in a square on a prepared sheet every time the colour was mentioned. If a story with objects was told the teams could be given a collection of the objects or pictures of the objects that they will be hearing in the story. When that particular object is named they have to produce its counterpart.

21

ST. MARY'S COLLEGE
FALLS ROAD, BELFAST 12.

7. *Absurdities*. Ask children to listen for things that sound silly or absurd in stories or sentences. Sentences with mistakes in them are read and the children have to point these out. The adult reads and the child responds.

> e.g. The sun is blue.
> Cook put the ice-cream to keep cold in the oven.
> I wrote the letter with my finger.
> The dog mooed when it was cross.

8. Tell a story for *drawing games* which gives some instructions in the form of a short story or description.

> e.g. In the kitchen there was a table. The table had a green cloth on it. On the cloth there was a cup and saucer. The cup was red and the saucer was yellow.

Ask the children to draw and colour the table and the things on it. Some children can only cope with a single sentence; other can be told quite a complicated story.

9. *Drawing a simpler version*. To make the above activity easier give duplicated pictures so that the children only have to remember the colours and colour in the objects.

B. *Visual memory and discrimination*

One should be careful not to make these solely pencil and paper games as these could be too difficult for some young learners. It would be better to start with active games or to use objects for some of the activities. (Many of the suggestions given can be found in other published materials.)

1. *Follow the leader*. Choose a leader, maybe the adult at first, and ask this person to make an action in some way. The children copy this trying to remember all the details. If the children work well together then one child can copy and the other children can point out if anything was forgotten at the end of the try.

2. **Kim's Game**. There are many variations of 'Kim's Game'. In this game the adult places a selection of objects on a table or tray and allows the players a certain amount of time to look and remember these. Then behind a screen or with the players blindfolded one or more objects are removed. It is slightly easier if a cover is put over the table or the tray and the objects withdrawn wrapped under the cover. The aim is to see how many of the removed objects can be recalled. It would be better to start with a few large objects on a table. When the children seem more proficient then many small objects can be used.

A variation of this game is to lay out the objects from left to right and then change the order of two or three of the objects. Ask the child to replace them in the correct order. Objects can also be added.

3. **Pelmanism** is a type of 'Kim's Game' which can be played with picture cards or playing cards. The cards are placed face downwards on the table and one player turns over two at a time. If a pair is shown the player gains it. If dissimilar cards are raised these are replaced in the same position. Some children are very adept at this game so the adult should be careful when pairing players.

4. ***Group the picture***. Give the children pictures of various vehicles, foods, clothes, animals etc. and ask them to group them according to their categories. Other variants could be according to size or colour.

5. ***Find the difference***. Prepare sets of pictures. Give at one time two similar cards and one that is different (e.g. two dogs and one cat) and ask the children to explain the differences.

6. ***Group the shape***. Prepare sets of shapes. Give the children sets of these cut-out shapes and ask the children to group them according to shape, design, size or colour.

7. *Match the shape.* The adult has a collection of shapes and so do the children. Hold up a particular shape for a very short time. Put it down and ask the children to remember and find the same.

8. *Draw the shape.* A variation would be drawing the shape. After a brief exposure the child has to reproduce this. Young children find using the black or white board more interesting. Other children can be asked to add their ideas after the chosen person has finished.

9. *Find the missing shape.* Prepare sets of unfinished objects. Make sure these are recognisable. Ask the children to find these and replace them or to draw them in.

  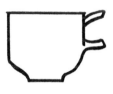

10. *Make the picture.* Prepare two duplicate pictures. Keep one in its original shape and cut the other into jigsaw pieces. (It is worth mounting these on card and covering them for future use.)

    Encourage the children to reconstruct the cut-up pictures to correspond with the uncut one. It is important to have pictures ranging from two or three simple parts to the complex arrangements found in commercial puzzles.

    A harder version would be to test the memory by taking away the uncut version after it has been studied so that there is no readily available model for the children to copy.

11. **Big or small.** Prepare worksheets that contain rows of lower case and capital letters. Ask the children to circle or highlight the big letters or the small letters.

e.g.	AAaa	aaaA	AAAa	aaaA	
CCC	Ccc	ccC	CCc	ccc	cCC
BBBB		BBBB	bbbb	bBbB	
DdD	DDd	ddd	DDD		
MmmM	mmMM	Mm	MMMM	mMmM	

12. **Match the word.** A more sophisticated variant of (7) 'match the shape' is to find and remember and reproduce a particular word.

13. **Draw the word.** This is another sophisticated variant of (8) 'draw the shape' and without children realising it they would be learning how to spell actual words. These would have to be short ones for young children or for those who have particularly poor short-term visual memories.

BE CAREFUL

This activity should only be given to those children who can form letters correctly without help. In fact, try not to ask children who have problems with pencil control to undertake written activities before they are really ready to.

14. **Detective work.** These activities involve children's observational powers. Produce pictures containing 'odd things' and deliberate mistakes and get the children to mark these in some way. Highlighter pens are useful here.

15. *Visual discrimination activities.* Many commercial worksheets are produced for visual discrimination purposes but it is also easy to prepare one's own. Ask the children to study the first shape carefully and then find its counterpart in the list. These can range from very simple pictures of objects to groups of letters.

on	an no on oon na un
flat	lfat talf aflt flat flot
daddy	babby dabby dabdy daddy dadby
803428	803248 802348 803428 248803
paged	pegad daged paged dgaep paedg

Stage 2
Semi-phonemic

In this stage children begin to make some sense of the sounds they are learning and hearing and to transfer these sounds to the written word. Often they can only correctly write one or two letters of any particular word, but because they know the word is longer they will add a random string of letters. Sometimes words will be represented by letters that match their letter names (e.g. 'r' is used frequently when it is heard in a word. How many times is the word *after* spelt *rfter* and *ask* as *rsk*?). Children are beginning to understand the conventions of writing, that it goes from left to right and that there are spaces between the words. Also there are instances of mirror writing and reversals (e.g. *was/saw*). It is also in this stage that a core sight vocabulary is being built up both of commonly used words and high-interest words.

Figure 2

One	**bae**	**me**	**and**	**babr**	**was**	**a**	**base**
One	day	me	and	dad	made	a	boat
Me	**and**	**babr**	**m**	**a**	**wsor**	**dnra**	
Me	and	dad	made	a	water	wheel	
I	**endl**	**a**	**baine**	**buse**			
I	made	a	toy	boat			
Me	**and**	**babr**	**endl**	**a**	**onls**		
Me	and	dad	made	a	hole		

A Year 2 boy's free writing. After each sentence he read his attempts to his teacher. (The actual piece of writing was not suitable for reproduction.)

The *National Curriculum Key Stage 1* general requirements are again outlined:

'Pupils should be taught to:
• write each letter of the alphabet;
• use their knowledge of sound-symbol relationships and phonological patterns;
• recognise and use simple spelling patterns;
• write common letter strings within familiar and common words;
• spell commonly occurring simple words;
• spell words with common prefixes and suffixes'.

In Figure 2 writing goes from left to right with spaces between the words. There are known words: *one/me/and/a/I*. The writer has some knowledge of which sounds go with which letters (b/w/m although there is some b/d letter confusion). Random letters are used to indicate length of word as he has used single and groups of letters to represent whole words or parts of words (*wsor - babr - endl*).

The beginnings of phonic awareness and early core sight spelling vocabularies games and activities

This is a most important stage because here the learners start to become spellers.

Sight words

AIM It is intended that children begin to use their sight memories in order to remember and recall simple words that they need to use in their early attempts at writing.

1. *Rote learning*. All children should be encouraged to learn by sight rather than copy the short common words. (If a core sight vocabulary is to be learnt for use in early writing then the first 100 core words, the McNally and Murray list can be used or the *Breakthrough* words.) There are many two letter words that can be learnt by even the child with the weakest visual memory. Young children can be encouraged to look at a word on a card, remember the letter order, turn the card over and write the word from memory. (For a more detailed explanation of how to learn words in this way, see page 50.)

2. *Let's look at words*. This activity involves the adult and the child looking at the similarities and differences between words. The length of the words and heights of the letters are examined. Prepare worksheets which show the outline of words down one side of the page. The words which fit the outline are on the other side. Get the child to draw lines to join these or write the word in the shape.

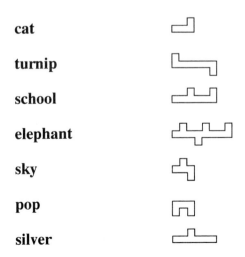

cat	
turnip	
school	
elephant	
sky	
pop	
silver	

If some children find this difficult then large examples can be made so that the child can actually pick up and fit the word into its outline.

3. ***Rote learning and matching.*** If there seem to be problems with learning simple words then use matching cards (a type of Pelmanism - see page 23 for an explanation of this activity) in order to make the children look carefully at words and their shapes. Use dissimilar words at first and then make the activity more difficult by using words that are similar in all but one letter (e.g. *house/horse, they/then* and *of/off*).

4. ***Finding the words for cloze stories.*** Cloze procedure is an activity which requires a space to be filled in by a word (either in writing or orally). Stories are written and/or read with some words omitted. Write some cloze procedure stories (or use stories already written in books) and read these out loud. These stories can be as simple as required. When a key or common word or known high-interest word is needed ask the child to find this from a prepared pile.

   e.g. Once upon a time there was a beautiful young _____
   called Cinderella who lived in an old house. She lived with
   her _____ and her two step-sisters. Cinderella's two
   sisters were so ugly that they were called the ugly sisters. Poor
   Cinderella was made to do all the work in the _____.
   She never went out and she had no friends.

Cards would be prepared with *house, father* and *girl.* Not only would the child have to listen and supply the word orally, the word would have to be found visually as well.

   If you tape the story, with each space given a number, give the children a sheet with the words on. The children must number these words to correspond with the numbered spaces.

5. *Oral cloze and writing*. The next stage would be to have a copy of the story and the gaps would be for words to be written in. These should be limited to known words. Therefore the above story could be written like this:

> e.g. Once upon a time there _____ a beautiful young girl called Cinderella who lived _____ an old house. She lived with her father _____ her two step-sisters. Cinderella's two sisters were so ugly _____ they were called the ugly sisters. Poor Cinderella was made to do _____ the work in the house. She never went out and she _____ no friends.

The words to be written in and spelt correctly would be *was, in, and, that, all, had.*

The National Curriculum spelling assessment uses this procedure at Key Stage 1 and children who have difficulties with spelling are found to feel more relaxed being tested in this way, especially if they are used to trying words for themselves.

One teacher has devised a story about a witch losing her friend which is read out loud by the adult. It has 40 spaces which coincide with all the spelling words on the Daniels and Diack spelling test. (This is a 40-word spelling test.) Depending on the ability of the children they are asked to write in either all the words dictated or those that are in sections A, B and/or C. The story is discussed afterwards. It has been found that Year 2 children are far more relaxed with this type of activity and some positively enjoy the story (however artificial it might seem). An example of this is:

>   (the)   (of)
> Rosie _____ wicked witch _____ the north
>   (lost)   (friend)
> _____ her best _____, Mabel . . . .
> . . . .   (date)
>   Whatever the _____

Mabel I can't wait,
(dart)
I'll throw a _____
So we're not apart.
Tiddly pooh
(do)
Come back _____.

(It should be recognised that because of the surrounding words which could give the children additional clues the scoring need not be as accurate as the originators intended. However, the purpose is to get some rough guide.)

5. *Finding and highlighting.* If children cannot read the words it will be difficult for them to learn to spell them. Therefore, before beginning to learn to spell the words, activities such as 'finding and highlighting' the word can be given first. Prepare worksheets with many words written on them, most of them containing the small word which is shown as the core word on the sheet. Get the children to highlight the small word whenever they can find it.

e.g. it	
little kitten wander	
bit item spitting	
spiteful cat	

The child highlights the 'it' in the words *little, bit, kitten, item, spitting, spiteful.*

6. *High-interest words.* Children should also be encouraged to learn by memory other words such as words that are of a high interest to them. These are words that are pertinent to them such as names of their family, their pets and their interests. They can choose particular words and make up their own word books which are 'words I can spell by myself'. Or they can make 'My Family' books where photographs and drawings contain captions written by the children.

8. *The Language Master*. This is a piece of equipment which takes a card with a magnetic strip at the bottom. The adult writes a word or a sentence on the card and has recorded what is written. The card slowly moves from left to right with the word being spoken at the same time. This can make the child more aware of the order of the letters. Some Language Masters also enable children to record what they are seeing and reading. (See Resources.)

9. *Concept Keyboard*. This is a special keyboard which is added to the computer. Whole words can be written on special sheets called overlays. But one must make sure that the children study and try to learn the words. The child presses the particular word and this then shows on the screen. The child can write whole sentences in this way. The Concept Keyboard is particularly helpful for enabling children to learn either common words or basic words from their reading schemes. (See Resources.)

Letter names

AIM To help children to learn the names of the letters of the alphabet when these are presented in any order.

1. *Alphabet lines and trails*. In order to teach letter names and their sequence, devise alphabet lines and trails. Start with a few letters at a time with children using plastic or wooden letters and matching against the written ones. When the child feels able to cope without the visual stimulus the written match should be taken away to see how much can be remembered. The names should be remembered at the same time as the shapes. Keep adding as letters are recalled. Magnetic letters can add interest because of their novelty value.

```
e.g.    a -------- b -------- c -------- d -------- e
        f -------- g -------- h -------- i -------- j
        j    d    h
        b    e    j    a
        c    f    g
```

2. *Speed trails*. Make the alphabet into shapes of animals or fruit and so on and encourage the children to join the letters in order. Organise speed trails against the clock or timer. Many of these activities can be made into team games with children sequencing the alphabet on wooden blocks or finding letters around the room and ordering them.

BE CAREFUL

Some children may learn the shapes of the letters without learning their names. Teachers must encourage oral naming when all these activities are undertaken.

3. *Hopscotch*. Get the children to chant the letter names while playing hopscotch with letters on the squares.

		e		
b	h	i	m	p
		c		
	d	g	f	
a	k	r	s	l
	j	n	t	
		o		

4. *Upper and lower case*. Devise similar activities with matching upper and lower case letters.

5. *Remembering letter shapes and names*. Teach letter names in rhymes and jingles as songs but be careful as this can result in rote memory without the shapes of the letters being known and associated with their label. It is helpful for the children to handle the letters but singing is always faster than handling.

6. *Dice and spinners*. To check if the names of the letters of the alphabet are completely known devise dice with letters on them or make spinners which are to be used for naming or matching games. Give children an alphabet chart or a trail and when they spin the spinner or shake the dice they name and mark on their chart whichever letter comes up.

7. *Alphabet bingo*. Make bingo boards and cards with letter names on them. Give the children the cards with letters and they cover the correct letter if they have this on their chart. Encourage the children to say the letter names as they place them.

   A variant is to have the board written with capital letters and the cards with lower case.

b	p	d	k
c	t	e	f
o	a	j	l
m	n	u	w

8. Play the oral games of **I pack my bag** or **I-spy** with letter names in order to match letter names with objects.

9. *Codes*. For older children with problems with letters, working with codes is effective. The adult makes a simple message but one that requires action of some sort.

e.g. a	b	c	d	e	f	g	h	i	j	k	l	m
1	2	3	4	5	6	7	8	9	10	11	12	13
n	o	p	q	r	s	t	u	v	w	x	y	z
14	15	16	17	18	19	20	21	22	23	24	25	26

7.15	1.14.4	7.5.20	1	16.5.14.3.9.12
(go	and	get	a	pencil)

Letter sounds

AIM To enable children to learn the common sounds for initial letters and short consonants when these are presented in their written form.

Similar games and activities can be organised for sounds as for letter names. Children sometimes need a pictorial clue for learning the particular sounds but whatever pictures are used make sure that the name of the picture shown is really understood by the child. For example, 'c' for cup could be labelled as *mug* by those children who do not have the word *cup* in their vocabularies. Go through the pictures first if there is any doubt about the children's knowledge.

1. *What is the sound?* It is helpful for children to identify as many of the common letter sounds as they can with other familiar sounds. Give these as riddles.

    e.g What sound do you make when you blow out a candle? *wh*
        What sound do you make when you ask someone
           to be quiet? *sh*
        What sound do you make when someone pinches you? *ow*
        What sound do you make when you are surprised? *o, ow*
        What sound does a dog make when he's angry? *gr*

2. *Rhyming snap, pairs and I-spy*. Devise rhyming word games such as rhyming snap, pairs or I-spy.

3. *Pictures and sounds*. Prepare picture sheets of commonly known objects. The child has to colour the pictures that begin with the particular sound written at the top of the sheet. Ending sounds can also be given but these are more difficult. Even harder are medial (middle) short vowels. Make sure that there are some pictures that are not applicable or else the child will colour all the pictures.

4. *Alphabetical oral games* can be fun with children thinking of an animal, its name, what it is like and what it eats.
   > e.g Danny the dog likes drawing and eating doughnuts.
   > Freddy the fish likes fencing and eating figs.
   > Timmy the tortoise likes training and eating tadpoles.
   > Mavis the mouse likes mountain climbing and eating meringues.
   This can work as a team game with actions. An alternative could be with the children introducing themselves using letters of their names.
   > e.g 'Exciting Emily' or 'Dirty Daniel' or 'Kind Kevin'.

5. *Oral activities*. Once rhyme is thoroughly understood then oral activities can be given to enable the child to hear which words are the 'odd ones out'. These can be initial letters or endings. It is difficult for some children to hear differences in the middle of words so this should not be tried too soon or the child may become confused.
   > e.g Which word doesn't sound the same as the others? Listen to the first sounds:
   >
   > | mat | man | mop | bun | mug |
   > |-----|-----|-----|-----|-----|
   > | jam | rot | jelly | Jane | Jill |

   or

   > Listen to the last sounds:
   >
   > | bat | cot | fit | rip | jet |
   > |-----|-----|-----|-----|-----|
   > | back | clock | hen | stick | peck |

6. *Making sense of text.* In order to hear words or parts of words, read out 'oral cloze' stories (see page 30, number 4). These can be as simple as is necessary with either nouns omitted or words at the end of sentences. An example of this could be *'Cinderella has to work very hard for her two ugly _____ '* or *'Jack climbed up the _____ to see what was at the top'*.

Encourage the children to produce the correct words or their own words that make sense.

7. *Oral cloze with first sound clues.* Sometimes give the first sound. This will limit the child's guesses.

e.g The children listened to their t_____ as she told a st_____.
It is well to remember that any work given orally/aurally on initial consonants should be as 'unvoiced' as possible. This means try to cut the consonant short without adding an extra sound (e.g. 't' not 'tu' or 'ter', 'st' not 'stu' or 'ster'). Children can wrongly form the impression that there are two letters making a single sound.

Stage 3
Phonemic
The core vocabulary of known sight words is built up and used but it is in this stage that phonic knowledge (knowledge of sounds) is transferred from one word to another. Each sound is represented by a letter. There are the beginnings of the understanding of syllabification with vowels being placed in each syllable. The main feature of this stage is that there is an over-dependence on the sounds rather than the visual appearance of the words. Some children remain locked into this mode of spelling as they seem to lack the self-confidence to trust their eyes rather than their ears.

Figure 3

Lait	one	**nite**	my	**frend**	woke	me	saying	
Late		night		friend				
wood	you	enjoy	a	**tryul**	run	in	my	new
would				trial				
hellikopter.	I	had		**skareseley**		**skrambulled**		
helicopter				scarcely		scrambled		
into	my	tracksuit		**befor**	we	were	away.	
				before				
The	**lites**	of	the	**sitee**	glowed	**beneeth,**	the	
	lights			city		beneath		
stars	above.							

Part of the Margaret Peters' diagnostic spelling assessment passage for 9/10-year-olds written by a Year 6 boy. (It is not possible to show this in its original form because of the teacher's marks and comments on it.)

In Figure 3 a sight vocabulary of both keywords and others is known and used. All unknown words are sounded out with much known phonic knowledge being transferred from one word to another (e.g. ite/ait/ood/end). He is coping with syllabification as each syllable contains a vowel (e.g. *hellikopter*/helicopter, *skareseley*/scarcely.)

The *National Curriculum Key Stage 2* general requirements are again outlined.

'Pupils should be taught to:
- spell complex, polysyllabic words which conform to regular patterns, and how to break long and complex words into more manageable units, using their knowledge of meaning and word structure;
- memorise the visual patterns of words, including those which are irregular;
- recognise silent letters;
- use the apostrophe to spell shortened forms of words;
- use appropriate terminology, including vowel and consonant'.

'Children should be building their own bank of words which they can spell correctly, using their dictionary skills, using their letter knowledge for alternative ways of spelling and patterning and using their word knowledge to understand the relevance of roots and origins. They should be taught to use common prefixes and suffixes, about word families and about words with inflectional endings'.

In Figure 3 the writer has learnt many common words (*one, me, into, had, new* etc.). Monosyllabic words such as *track, stars* and *glowed* are correctly written and he has attempted to use his knowledge of letter patterns to spell *lait, frend, nite, lites, wood* and *beneeth.*

Getting prepared for sounds games and activities

Many published spelling schemes use sound patterns as their way into learning spelling. Unfortunately children are too often left to complete the worksheets for themselves and they do this by visual methods. They look at the particular pattern and just use the page as a 'filling-in' activity. In this way correct results are obtained but the children neither commit the words to their memories nor do they speak the sounds (either internally or orally). Therefore, it should not be surprising when these children do not transfer their phonic knowledge from one word to another because, of course, this has not been internalised.

So, any games or activities undertaken in this section must either be completely oral or written answers should be checked orally at frequent intervals.

Spelling by sounds

AIM To equip children with the means of attempting to spell words using common sound patterns and to use their growing knowledge of sound patterns to attempt unknown words.

1. *Using paper and pencil.* There are many paper and pencil activities that can be devised as long as the adults are aware of the possible problems that have been mentioned above. Draw balloons or ice-creams

or flowers (in fact any shape or object) with a sound pattern outside and a single initial consonant inside. The children have to write in and say their new word.

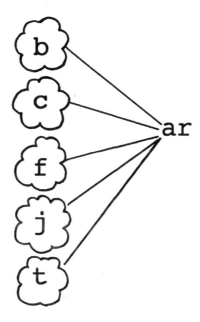

There are many variations on changing the word by the initial sound. Much has been written about this type of procedure by the educators Bryant and Bradley (see References). The initial sound is termed the 'onset' and the block of sound following this is termed the 'rime'. For example, the word *house* can be divided into *h + ouse* and the word *dog* into *d + og*. All these activities involve changing the word/making a word/matching a word/reading a word using sounds. One should not confuse children by adding the odd word that does not follow the sound pattern (e.g. *hat/sat/that/cat/chat* but not *what*). This will be added later when the child is confident at one particular activity.

2. **Word chains, word ladders** and **word staircases** can be made for this activity. Plastic, wooden or magnetic letters are useful here so that

the child can physically alter words. If the consonants are in one colour and the vowels in another then this helps children to understand the different functions of these letters. Divide the children into groups or teams so that they can discuss the words they have made. (If the adult is concerned about the types of words that can be made then some sounds will have to be avoided such as *um* and *it*!)

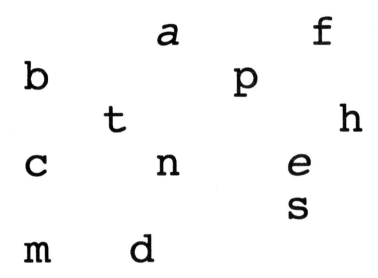

3. *Spot the vowel.* Use coloured wooden, magnetic or plastic letters (vowels in blue and consonants in red) and make a collection of real objects (e.g. a cat, a fan, a pan). The children spell the object's name using the letters and begin to understand the purpose of the blue letter. Then they can change either the blue or red letters to make other words (e.g. *fin/pin* or *cat/fat/fit* or *ran/man/mat*.)

4. *Hear the vowel.* Make boards with six spaces and write two vowels three times each in the squares. Start with vowels that sound very different as with 'i' and 'o' and then use those that confuse such as 'a' and 'u'. Gather a collection of picture cards which are of simple words with the vowels in the middle. Ask the child to take a picture

and say it and place it on its correct square. If this is difficult for the child then say the word yourself so that the child can hear good enunciation.

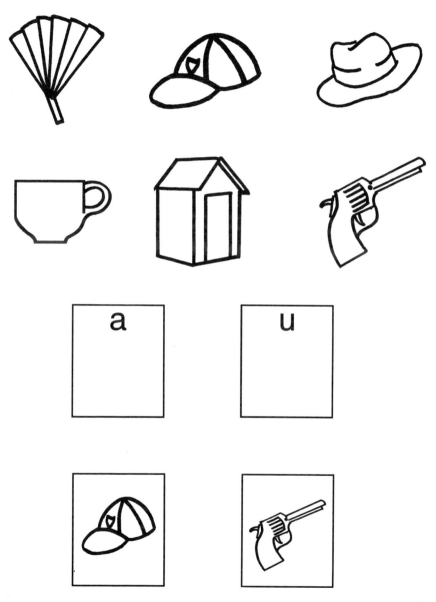

5. **Which is it?** Make worksheets of pictures with commonly confusing sounds. At the top of each sheet write 'which is it?' and the letters. Ask the child to say each word and write the correct letter underneath. This activity helps children with speech problems and is an activity that will bridge using hearing sounds with seeing the correct letters.

6. **'Attack' with pictures.** 'Attack' is a very structured system for teaching spelling. It relies on children building up their phonic knowledge. (See Richards, J, 1988, in References for details.) Make supplementary worksheets using initial consonants, medial vowels and final consonants. Instead of expecting the children to make words themselves, give them a stimulus word orally or a picture and they can spell the word by using the given letters. Ask the children to make and write the words next to the pictures.

7. **Linking words.** Give simple cvc (consonant-vowel-consonant) words or even simple consonant blend (two consonants together such as 'bl' and 'gr') words which can be linked. Ask the child to draw the linked pair.

   e.g.   fat   chin
          ten   men
          thick   cat
          thin   brick

8. Devise card or board games which help with sounds. Make a set of **sound dominoes** where the child has to say the new word as well as fit it to the last domino. Devise **'post-it'** games where particular sound words are put into the correct slots. **Sound snap** and **sound pelmanism** are other alternatives.

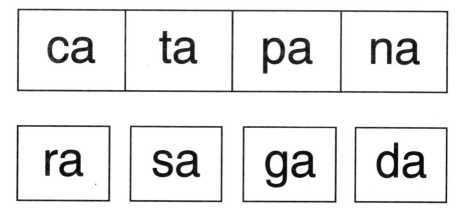

9. More sophisticated **board games** can involve dice and moving along from square to square with bonuses for reading particular sounds.

10. Make a 'sound' version of **Snakes and Ladders**. Number the 100 squares in the usual way and put in a selection of snakes and ladders. At the bottom of each ladder write a 'sound' word and in order to climb the ladder the player has to find a rhyming card from a pack (either a word or picture) and say it correctly. Snakes are used in the usual way and there can be bonus squares for extra moves. Here the player might have to spell a particular 'sound' word.

11. Not all games need boards or paper and pencil. There are **oral games** that will involve groups or the whole class. Divide the class into teams in the hall and give each team a 'rime' or sound unit. Say an 'onset' or beginning letter and if the team can make a word with this then one team member runs to the far end of the room. If two words can be made then two children can run and so on. More beginnings are given until the winning team's members have all made a word.

12. *Provide a rhyme*. Here children say rhyming words after a stimulus word is given. A variant of this would be adding a rhyme until no more can be given. The game continues until only one person is left in.

e.g.	stimulus	response	response	response	response
	crack	stack	back	whack	track

13. *'I-Spy'* with rhymes is another variant.
    e.g. I spy with my little eye something rhyming with curl.
    (answer = girl)

14. Make *oral poems* and use *'rap'* with rhyme. Rap is a rhythmic form of verse turned into a song with a definite beat which is 'chanted' rather than made into a tune and is usually about current issues. Children can make up rhymes about their favourite football teams, pop stars, sports or lessons with a drum beat or a xylophone accompaniment.

15. ***Bridging the gap between sound and sight.*** If the particular group of children undertaking these activities is secure in phonic knowledge then the beginnings of the 'odd' words can be shown. Children who supply *got/dot/lot/cot/pot* and then *what* as an oral/aural activity can be shown the discrepancy in *what* by writing these down. The more children become interested in words the more they can find words that do not follow the sound patterns. This will make them become aware of the make-up of words and will start bridging the gap between the phonemic and transitional stages of spelling acquisition.

16. Other activities for this section are about **syllables** where children can tap out and say the number of 'parts' they can hear in words. Their names are best for this at first and after they have understood this make a class register showing the names with the first (or only) syllable coloured in one colour, the second in another and so on.

e.g.	1	2	3	4
	A<u>nn</u>	Da<u>vid</u>	Benjam<u>in</u>	Elizab<u>eth</u>
	D<u>avid</u>	Jen<u>ny</u>	Gilli<u>an</u>	
	Je<u>nny</u>	Benj<u>am</u>in	Eliz<u>a</u>beth	
	Ben<u>j</u>amin	Gill<u>i</u>an		
	Gil<u>li</u>an	El<u>iz</u>abeth		
	E<u>liz</u>abeth			

Rhythmic activities are very useful and will stand the children in good stead for later spelling of polysyllabic words. One example is that the children can be grouped into three teams: one for three syllables, one for four and the other for five. A prepared story which has a suitable selection of multi-syllabic words is read very slowly and the teams have to indicate in some way when one of their words is given.

Stage 4
Transitional
The English language is not a truly phonemic one. Sounds can be represented by a variety of letters or clusters of letters, e.g. the sound

'or' can be written as 'au', 'aw', 'ough', 'oar'. Some words are so irregular that they can only be learnt visually. Therefore, children have to understand that they cannot rely on sounds alone but have to look, remember and recall what words actually look like if they are to become correct spellers. Therefore, this transitional stage is where the children start acquiring acceptable visual letter patterns. When moving from sounds to relying on the visual appearance it is possible for children to remember the letters but to place them in the wrong order in the word.

Figure 4

The	**machein** machine	touched	down	with	**pricition** precision	in
the	**rouf** rough	**mountinus** mountainous	**rejen** region	without	even	
scaping scraping	its	**serface.** surface	The	children	**surronded** surrounded	
the	pilot,	**owh** who	**explaned** explained	that	his	**oldimeter** altimeter
and	**tempercher** temperature	**gacg** gauge	were	damaged	and	he
was	**ankshius** anxious	about	increasing	**altitued** altitude	in	
these	**frezzing** freezing	**condisions.** conditions				

Part of Margaret Peters' diagnostic spelling assessment passage for 10/11-year-olds written by a Year 9 boy. (As with the other examples of children's work it has not been possible to reproduce the original piece of writing.)

In Figure 4 there are signs that the pupil is relying on his visual memory and by doing so sometimes misses out letters or muddles their order (e.g. *scaping/machien/owh*). His words communicate and he is attempting to use correct letter sequences (e.g. *'sion*/tion' and *'ius*/ious').

It is asserted that the transitional stage can last up to six years. If it has taken some children more than the very early years of their education to work through the early stages, from pre-communicative to the phonemic, then there will be children in their secondary years who will still be working through the stages, especially stages 3 and 4, and consolidating their learning. (This fact can be seen by Figure 4's example.) Many secondary teachers are unaware of this and so incorrectly judge their pupils' attainments.

The *National Curriculum Key Stage 2* general requirements are again outlined.

'Pupils should be taught to:

* spell complex, polysyllabic words which conform to regular patterns, and how to break long and complex words into more manageable units, using their knowledge of meaning and word structure;
* memorise the visual patterns of words, including those which are irregular;
* recognise silent letters;
* use the apostrophe to spell shortened forms of words;
* use appropriate terminology, including vowel and consonant'.

'Children should be building their own bank of words which they can spell correctly, using their dictionary skills, using their letter knowledge for alternative ways of spelling and patterning and using their word knowledge to understand the relevance of roots and origins. They should be taught to use common prefixes and suffixes, about word families and about words with inflectional endings'.

In Figure 4 the writer is spelling common words correctly (e.g. *down, even, were, about*) and is using his knowledge of some words with common patterns to make other words (e.g. *touched* and *rouf* and *er* and *ane*). He also has the knowledge of the prefixes *'tion'* and *'sion'*.

Activities to help children become aware of the visual make-up of words
There is always the danger that when children are learning by sight memory they fail to do so because they copy the stimulus word rather

than committing it to memory. Any game or activity involving sight memory and recall must make sure that the children learn not to 'cheat'.

Some of the activities are extensions of those previously described. The decision as to where to start and what exactly to provide always depends on the age and competence of the learner.

Much of the memory work involves the *LOOK - COVER - WRITE - CHECK* procedure that has been written about by Margaret Peters and well-documented by Charles Cripps in his work on spelling (see References). Children are expected to look at the word and memorise its spelling, then cover the word and write it without copying. They then check to see if they have spelt it correctly. However, it seems that it is more helpful to add extra functions to the sequence. The procedure should be lengthened to *LOOK - COVER - REMEMBER - SAY - WRITE - CHECK - RECORD - REVISE*. This enables the learners to understand that words have to be put into their memories and to be revised until the words can be automatically written on all occasions.

The learner is being encouraged to look closely at words and here more paper and pencil or highlighter activities involving this should be devised.

Spelling by sight memory

AIM To encourage and enable children to use their visual memories for learning to spell new words and to associate words that have similar visual patterns.

Because it can be difficult for some children to learn the many irregular words in the English spelling system, some extra ways of remembering should be offered. Here the multi-sensory programmes are necessary where the child handles letters (using wooden or plastic letters), writes letters, says the letter names and remembers the sequence inside the word.

1. *Finding words and patterns*. Nominate words or patterns of letters and instruct the child to find these on a magazine page, around the

room, on food packets etc. Even going around the shops can bring
about this activity.

e.g.	or	it	in	as
	Woolworths	Littlewoods	Sainsburys	Asda
		Smiths		

on	her	he
Dillons	Mothercare	Mothercare

2. *Finding a look-alike*. A variant is to give a word and ask the child
to search for those that look like it or are exactly the same.

    e.g. had

       hat, ham, has, hall, hash, had, have, haw,

       hack, happy, hay, hand

3. *Word searches*. Construct word searches but be wary of any that
make the child look in any way other than left to right. The children
have to be quite competent if they are asked to cope with words running
diagonally or back to front.

4. *'Hangman'* is not a particularly good activity for helping correct
sequencing as the letters are not placed in order. However, this game
can be played successfully by building up words using letters from
left to right. If the word chosen is *elephant,* give the starting letter
and the spaces, e _ _ _ _ _ _ _, and only when the 'l' is given is this
written in. Then wait until the next 'e' and so on. Try to use words
that have some phonically regular structure so that the children can
guess from sounds as well as check visually.

5. *Words in words*. The next stage from being aware of patterns in
words and words that look similar is finding smaller words in longer
ones. Give children lists of words and get them to write down those
they can find. One can begin with personal words such as names
before going on to any longer words. The children do not have to

learn to spell the words nor even to be able to read the long one. They just have to use their visual powers to find shorter words. One should note that these smaller words must have their letter order in the same sequence as they are in the longer word.

e.g.	Christopher	=	is	stop	to	top	he	her
	interest	=	in	rest				
	important	=	port	or	an	ant		
	teacher	=	tea	teach	each	ache	he	her
	sentence	=	sent	ten				
	worker	=	work	or				

Taking letters out of order in words to make other words is a different activity and is only for the competent speller.

6. *Car number plates*. On car journeys, car number plates make children aware of letter order by getting them to decide on words that have the letters in them in the same order but with other letters in between. This is a sophisticated activity but is particularly useful for trying to visualise words. (For example, the letters *MNC* could conjure up the word *magnetic*.)

7. *TV recall*. When watching TV the advertisements show names of products and other words very quickly so encourage children to see how much of a word they can recall by writing it down.

8. *Letter strings with paper and pencil*. Devise similar paper and pencil activities with letter strings as with sound patterns (see page 40, number 1). This time, of course, it does not matter if the words do not sound the same (e.g. *bread/dead/meadow/bead/read/lead)*. Both pronunciations are acceptable.

9. The *board and card games* can also follow similar rules to those made for the sound pattern words.

10. **Word sums**. Make multisyllabic words by adding words together as in word sums. Pair each word on the left with a word from the right column to make a new word.

e.g.

sun	port
stair	room
class	shine
car	case

11. **Mnemonics**. Making up mnemonics (which is a system of rules to aid the memory) can help to retain troublesome words (e.g. *I put some water in charlie's hat = Ipswich*). This activity should not be over-encouraged or it could mean that the child spends more time thinking up a particular clue when the actual word could be learnt more easily.

12. **Strange pronunciations**. Also for troublesome words 'saying words funny' or saying words as they are spelt can be employed (e.g. *friend = fri/end* and *Wednesday = wed/nes/day*).

13. **Contractions**. Show the children how the two full words are linked and get them to work some out themselves.

didn't	=	did not
can't	=	cannot
isn't	=	is not

There are ways into learning like Simultaneous Oral Spelling, Cued-spelling and Precision Spelling techniques that are outside the scope of this book. Some children will need a personal card rather than a word book so that keywords or topic words can be readily accessed. A class thesaurus for particular subject areas is also useful. However, these do not readily form a game or activity in the sense this book has offered so far. Some of the books in the Reference section give ideas about learning spelling.

Stage 5
Correct

This heading does not mean that every word will be correctly spelt but that the children will have taken on board all the correct strategies for spelling acquisition and will be applying them as precisely as they are able. Because of their growing awareness of correct letter patterns in words children will be able to look at their attempts to 'see' if they look correct or not and if unsure they will try alternatives until the right one is recognised. Children will apply the known spelling patterns to syllables in polysyllabic words and will use spelling patterns logically to unknown words. Of course these will not always be accurate but if the learners are interested in words then trial and error will be rewarded.

Figure 5

nurv	peo	son	m
nurve	pere	sona	maind
neere	pair	soner	miad
nerve		soona	miand
nearv		sooner	mind

Four words from the Schonell spelling test showing attempts made by a Year 9 girl. Whenever she recognised a word that looked incorrect to her she would say 'it doesn't look right' and would make several attempts until she was sure of the correctness.

To refer back to the problems some children have with their auditory and/or visual memories it can be seen that particular problems could occur at stages 3 and 4. Those children who find coping with sounds very difficult could have no phonic strategies whereas those with exclusively secure auditory memories will rely totally on sounding out words.

For those children with both memories flawed, their spelling can be very haphazard and inefficient because of their inability to communicate with the reader. Many children with specific learning difficulties have problems with both memory functions and for them it is very necessary to build up some structured strategies for attempting words when they are writing. Often these children will not get to the 'correct' stage in spelling and will function at a Key Stage behind their actual ages or at the early parts of a particular Key Stage. Helping children with specific learning difficulties means much over-learning and repetition and as much home-school liaison as is possible. Many of the activities and games in the early stages are very suitable for these children although some will have to be adapted depending on the children's ages.

The *National Curriculum Key Stage 3* general requirements are again outlined. The spelling acquisition that has been learnt in the previous Key Stages is to be built on. Pupils should be helped to increase their knowledge of regular patterns of spelling, word families, roots of words and their derivations. They should be taught to spell increasingly complex polysyllabic words that do not conform to regular patterns, and to proofread their writing carefully to check for errors using dictionaries where appropriate. Pupils should be given opportunities to develop discrimination in relation to other complexities in spelling, including heteronyms, e.g. *minute, lead, wind,* and sight rhymes, e.g. *tough, dough.*

Figure 5 does not show the full extent of the writer's attempts at spelling but it does show that although she has particular difficulties with spellings she is becoming aware of patterns in words and an awareness of word families. She also tries to check her accuracy.

Becoming proficient at spelling games and activities

By this stage children should be well aware of how words are made up both by sound and letter patterns. If by this time they attempt all unknown words and use both communicable and reasonably correct attempts and if they can see that some of their attempts are not totally correct then they are well on their ways to becoming proficient spellers. However, there are still games and activities rather than just learning spellings that can be undertaken.

Becoming more proficient at spelling

AIM To give children an awareness of the structure and make-up of words in the English language.

1. *Syllabification.* Some children telescope words when they try longer ones. Get them to beat out and say the syllables as they try to write the multi-syllabic word. Children can 'test' each other by thinking of a long word, stating how many syllables it has and then trying to spell it. If children are encouraged to be interested in words then they can be helped with how words are structured. They can be told that each syllable has a vowel or vowel combination (and that can include a 'y').

2. *Building words.* In order to help with multi-syllabic words, prepare cards with these words written quite large and then cut them in their relevant parts. Get the child to word build. Start with a few words and then add to these. Sometimes use words that can have alternative endings such as 'ing', 'ed', 'er' etc.

in   spect   ed

ing   in   tend

pre   form   er

3. *Cutting the word.* As an alternative to number 2, prepare cards as above but ask the children to cut them where they believe the correct place is. In this way you can see if the children have started to understand the structure of words.

pretender   informing

inspector

4. *Structure of words*. Help children to learn about the structure of words. Following on from 2 and 3, children can start to understand about root words and how suffixes and prefixes change their meanings. These 'additions' can be learnt as visual units so that children can start spelling more sophisticated words. Give a short root word and ask children, either singly or in pairs, to see how many words they can make by adding endings or beginnings. Those who are reasonable readers can check their attempts in a dictionary.

e.g. play	clean	invent	grace
plays	cleans	invents	graceful
played	cleaner	inventor	gracefully
playing	cleaning	inventing	disgrace
playful	unclean	invention	disgraceful
playfully			disgracefully
playground			
playpen			

Those children who are fairly competent with their written work could write some of their words into sentences to show the meanings.

5. *Word derivations*. Teach the children about the origins of words. Some are derived from old languages. Others are actually foreign words which have been assimilated into English. Older children can be given tasks to find words such as these or they can be given the word and by using the dictionary find out all they can about it.

   e.g. derivations of words such as 'tele'
   foreign words such as *spaghetti*

Slowly and surely children can learn what is the most probable way of spelling a word. There are certain 'rules' that can be given but because most have an exception one must be careful here.

Activities in this stage become more 'grown-up' as many children are more concerned with the content of their written work rather than of the process of spelling. Writing quickly to get thoughts on paper can often find the writer making mistakes that otherwise would not have occurred.

Proof reading should be encouraged and also marking of their own work. Proof reading needs to occur twice. The first for the reader to look for spelling errors and the second for the content. Proof reading is a skill which needs to be taught. Because children can read their own errors they may skim over these and miss them when reading through their work again. In order to pay attention to each word they should be encouraged to read from the final word back to the beginning. In this way they will have to look closely at each word and, therefore, will be more likely to pick out any mistake. This is long and tedious but it will prove helpful. If children feel secure in their peers then a friend could become the marker. Because children have more knowledge about words then '***try pads***' should be given for quick scribbling attempts.

Many activities should be concerned with the written message so that spelling becomes a simultaneous or even an incidental activity. Children should be encouraged to write messages and all types of writing activities should be employed. These are beyond the scope of this book but some helpful books are listed in Further Reading.

Conclusion

There is no guarantee that all children are going to become good spellers. One only has to ask colleagues about their own spelling abilities to see that the English language can continue to hold many mysteries. What we need to do is to take away the frightening aspects of learning to spell, to enable children to approach this skill with pleasure rather than pain, with interest rather than boredom.

The games and activities mentioned throughout this book are there to serve as a flavouring to sprinkle onto the more solid diet of actually *learning* spellings. They are to be used to help with the foundations of the written word and to help overcome any problems that might occur.

Children should not be denied the place of games and activities in their spelling acquisition. Their memories may be weak and their subsequent written work far from perfect but if they enjoy writing for writing's sake and have been liberated from at least one of the secretarial skills necessary for producing work that can be read by others, then our teaching has been successful. And if parents can be helped to understand this, then they may look on completion of written work as their child's success rather than over-concentrating on the correct way to spell a word.

References

Bradley, L and Bryant, P (1985) *Children's Reading Problems*, Blackwell.

Cripps, C (1991) *A Hand for Spelling*, LDA.

Daniels, J C and Diack, H (1960) *The Standard Reading Tests*, Chatto and Windus.

Gentry, J R (1981) 'Learning to spell developmentally' *Reading Teacher*, 34.4.

Mackay, D, Thompson, B and Schaub, P (1970) *Breakthrough to Literacy: Teachers' Manual*, Longman.

McNally, J and Murray, M (1985) *Key Words to Literacy*, School Master Publishing Company.

Peters, M L (1979) *Spelling: Caught or Taught - A New Look*, Routledge and Kegan Paul.

Peters, M L and Smith, B (1993) *Spelling in Context - Strategies for Teachers and Learners*, NFER-Nelson.

Richards, J (1988) *Attack Your Reading, Writing, Spelling Problems - Our Way*.

SCAA (1994) *The National Curriculum Orders, Programmes of Study, English*.

Resources and Further Reading

Alston, Jean (1992) *Spelling Helpline,* Dextral Books.

Alston, Jean (1995) *Assessing and Promoting Writing Skills,* NASEN.

Bentley, D (1990) *Teaching Spelling,* Reading and Language Centre, University of Reading.

Buttriss, J and Callander, A (1990) *Spellbound,* The AT Work Publishing Company Ltd.

CONCEPT KEYBOARD: *see* Concept Keyboard Special 1995
MAPE Software, Technology Centre, Newman College, Bartley Green, Birmingham B32 3NT
or
The Concept Keyboard Company, Unit 6, Moorside Road, Winnall Industrial Estate, Hampshire SO23 7RX.

Cripps, C (1991) *A Hand for Spelling Pupil Profile,* LDA.

SPELLMASTER: Elementary Spellmasters and Spellcheckers
Electronic Learning Products
The Mill House, Stanford Dingley, Reading, Berkshire RG7 7LS.

Hip Pocket Spelling Games (1978) Harcourt Brace Jovanovich (O/P).

LANGUAGE MASTER: Drake Educational Associates, St. Fagans Road, Fairwater, Cardiff CF5 3AE.

Let's Look (Visual Discrimination Activities), LDA.

Torbe, M (1988) *Teaching Spelling,* Ward Lock.